The Insider's Guide to Real Estate Success

Secrets of Top Performers Revealed

NELLA BYRAN

Copyright

No part of this should be reproduced without the permission of the author.

© Nella Byran 2024

Contents

Introduction 4

Unlocking the Door 8

Mindset Mastery 12

The Art of Analysis 16

Secrets of Selection: Finding Properties with Maximum Potential 20

Deal-Making Dynamics 24

The Power of Partnerships 28

From Acquisition to Activation 32

Revenue Streams Unveiled 36

Risk Management Redefined 40

Marketing Magic: Techniques for Effective Property Promotion 45

Customer Connection 49

Innovation Incubator 53

Growing Your Portfolio with Precision 57

Financial Fitness 62

Legacy Planning: Building a Sustainable Real Estate Empire 66

The Road Ahead 70

Reflections from the Top Performers in Real Estate 74

Conclusion 78

Introduction

Are you ready to unlock the secrets to real estate success and join the ranks of top performers in the industry? Welcome to "The Insider's Guide to Real Estate Success: Secrets of Top Performers Revealed." This book isn't just another guide to buying and selling properties—it's your comprehensive roadmap to mastering the art and science of real estate, crafted by those who have not only achieved success but have thrived in this dynamic and competitive field.

In this groundbreaking guide, we delve deep into the strategies, mindsets, and techniques employed by the industry's elite. From the moment you turn the first page, you'll embark on a transformative journey, beginning with "Unlocking the Door: Introduction to Insider Real Estate Strategies." Here, you'll gain invaluable insights into the mindset required to thrive in the real estate world, setting the stage for your journey towards unparalleled success.

As you progress through the chapters, you'll discover the keys to mindset mastery, cultivating the mentality of a top performer, and honing the art of analysis to decipher market trends and uncover lucrative opportunities. From selecting properties with maximum potential to mastering the dynamics of deal-making and negotiation, each chapter unveils the closely guarded secrets of the industry's most successful individuals.

But real estate success isn't achieved in isolation—it's about forging powerful partnerships and leveraging collaborative opportunities. "The Power of Partnerships" explores how strategic alliances can amplify profitability and propel you towards your goals with greater efficiency and effectiveness.

From acquisition to activation, you'll learn how to transform properties into profits, exploring diverse revenue streams and innovative marketing techniques to maximize returns. But success in real estate isn't without its challenges. That's why we delve into risk management strategies, ensuring you're equipped to navigate uncertainties and mitigate potential setbacks along the way.

Moreover, as technology continues to reshape the real estate landscape, "Innovation Incubator" unveils the latest advancements and how to harness them to your advantage. Whether it's scaling your portfolio with precision or optimizing financial resources for long-term wealth, each chapter is packed with actionable insights and practical advice to propel your success to new heights.

But beyond mere financial gain lies the opportunity to leave a lasting legacy. "Legacy Planning" explores how to build a sustainable empire that transcends generations, ensuring your impact on the real estate world endures long into the future.

As you reach the final chapters, you'll reflect on the road traveled and gain invaluable wisdom from the top performers themselves. Their insights, shared in "Closing Thoughts," serve as a reminder that while the journey to real estate success may be challenging, it's also immensely rewarding.

So, are you ready to embark on this transformative journey? The path to real estate success awaits—let's begin.

Unlocking the Door

As you progress through this chapter, you'll gain a deeper appreciation for the multifaceted nature of real estate success and the strategic approach required to unlock its full potential. Armed with these insider insights and strategies, you'll be well-equipped to embark on your journey towards becoming a top performer in the world of real estate. So, are you ready to unlock the door to your real estate success? Let's begin the journey together.

"Unlocking the Door" serves as the foundational cornerstone upon which your journey to real estate success begins. In this chapter, we lay the groundwork for understanding the intricate dynamics of the real estate industry and introduce you to the fundamental strategies employed by top performers.

At its core, real estate is not just about buying and selling properties—it's about understanding the market, mastering negotiation tactics, and cultivating a mindset geared towards success. This chapter delves deep into the mindset required to thrive in the competitive world of real estate, emphasizing the importance of ambition, resilience, and a relentless pursuit of excellence.

One of the key insights you'll uncover in this chapter is the notion that success in real estate is not solely determined by external factors such as market conditions or economic trends. Instead, it is largely influenced by your internal mindset and belief system. By adopting the mentality of a top performer—characterized by unwavering determination, a growth mindset, and a commitment to continuous learning—you'll position yourself for success from the outset.

We explore the concept of strategic thinking and how it can be applied to every aspect of your real estate endeavors. From identifying lucrative investment opportunities to negotiating favorable deals, strategic thinking enables you to anticipate challenges, mitigate risks, and capitalize on emerging trends.

Central to unlocking the door to real estate success is the ability to develop a comprehensive understanding of the market. This includes analyzing market trends, assessing property values, and identifying areas of growth and opportunity. By mastering the art of analysis, you'll gain a competitive edge in navigating the complexities of the real estate landscape and making informed investment decisions.

Furthermore, this chapter emphasizes the importance of setting clear goals and developing a strategic plan to achieve them. Whether your objective is to build a diversified portfolio, generate passive income, or achieve financial independence, having a well-defined roadmap is essential for realizing your aspirations.

In addition to mindset and strategic thinking, we also explore the critical role of networking and relationship-building in the world of real estate. Cultivating strong connections with industry professionals, investors, and potential clients not only expands your opportunities but also enhances your credibility and reputation within the industry.

Mindset Mastery

By the end of this chapter, you'll emerge with a newfound sense of clarity, confidence, and determination to cultivate the mindset of a top performer in the real estate industry. Armed with these powerful insights and strategies, you'll be well-equipped to overcome obstacles, seize opportunities, and achieve your goals with unwavering conviction. So, are you ready to embark on the journey of mindset mastery and unlock your full potential for real estate success? Let's begin the transformation together.

"Mindset Mastery: Cultivating the Mentality of a Top Performer" is a transformative journey into the psychological landscape of real estate success. In this pivotal section of "The Insider's Guide to Real Estate Success," we delve deep into the mindset that distinguishes top performers from the rest, and we provide you with the tools and strategies to cultivate that mindset within yourself.

At its core, mindset mastery is about harnessing the power of your thoughts, beliefs, and attitudes to propel you towards your goals. We begin by debunking common myths surrounding success in real estate, emphasizing that it's not just about luck or innate talent, but rather about adopting the right mindset and habits.

One of the key principles explored in this chapter is the concept of a growth mindset, as popularized by psychologist Carol Dweck. A growth mindset is characterized by a belief in the ability to learn and improve over time, viewing failures and setbacks as opportunities for growth rather than insurmountable obstacles. Through real-life examples and practical exercises, we guide you in shifting from a fixed mindset to a growth mindset, unlocking your full potential for success in the real estate industry.

Also, we explore the importance of resilience and perseverance in the face of challenges. Real estate is a highly competitive and often unpredictable field, requiring resilience to weather the inevitable ups and downs. By adopting a resilient mindset, you'll be better equipped to bounce back from setbacks, adapt to changing circumstances, and ultimately thrive in the face of adversity.

Another crucial aspect of mindset mastery is the cultivation of confidence and self-belief. Confidence is not just about being assertive or outgoing; it's about having faith in your abilities and trusting yourself to navigate the complexities of the real estate market. Through practical strategies and mindset-shifting techniques, we empower you to cultivate unwavering confidence and self-assurance in your real estate endeavors.

Furthermore, we explore the importance of goal setting and visualization in shaping your mindset for success. By setting clear, actionable goals and visualizing your desired outcomes, you'll create a roadmap for achievement and instill a sense of purpose and direction in your real estate journey.

In addition to individual mindset mastery, we also highlight the importance of surrounding yourself with a supportive community of like-minded individuals. Whether it's through mentorship, mastermind groups, or networking events, connecting with others who share your aspirations and values can provide invaluable support, inspiration, and accountability on your path to success.

The Art of Analysis

By the end of this chapter, you'll emerge with a comprehensive understanding of the art of analysis in real estate and the strategies required to decipher market trends and identify lucrative opportunities. Armed with these insights and techniques, you'll be well-equipped to make informed investment decisions, capitalize on emerging trends, and achieve sustainable success in the dynamic world of real estate. So, are you ready to master the art of analysis and unlock the door to unlimited opportunities in real estate? Let's dive in and uncover the secrets together.

Here, we unveil the critical skills and insights necessary to navigate the complex and ever-evolving landscape of the real estate market. In this chapter, we delve deep into the strategies and techniques employed by top performers to effectively analyze market trends and identify lucrative opportunities.

At its core, the art of analysis in real estate involves gathering and interpreting data to make informed decisions about investments, acquisitions, and sales. We begin by emphasizing the importance of staying abreast of current market trends and economic indicators, providing you with the tools and resources needed to conduct thorough market research.

One of the key components of market analysis is understanding the local market dynamics. Whether you're investing in residential properties, commercial real estate, or land development, each market has its own unique characteristics and trends that must be carefully evaluated. Through detailed case studies and real-world examples, we illustrate how to identify emerging trends, assess market demand, and anticipate future growth opportunities.

Moreover, we explore the role of data analytics and technology in modern real estate analysis. From sophisticated market research tools to predictive modeling algorithms, advancements in technology have revolutionized the way we analyze and interpret real estate data. By leveraging these tools and techniques, you'll gain a competitive edge in identifying undervalued properties, predicting market fluctuations, and maximizing returns on your investments.

In addition to quantitative analysis, we also emphasize the importance of qualitative factors in real estate decision-making. This includes considerations such as demographic trends, zoning regulations, infrastructure development, and socioeconomic indicators, all of which can have a significant impact on property values and investment prospects.

Furthermore, we delve into the concept of risk management in real estate analysis. While every investment carries inherent risks, effective risk management involves identifying potential pitfalls and implementing strategies to mitigate them. Whether it's conducting thorough due diligence, diversifying your investment portfolio, or hedging against market volatility, we provide you with the tools and techniques needed to safeguard your investments and minimize downside risk.

Secrets of Selection: Finding Properties with Maximum Potential

By the end of this chapter, you'll emerge with a newfound mastery of property selection and the ability to uncover properties with unparalleled potential. Armed with these insider secrets and strategies, you'll be well-equipped to navigate the complexities of the real estate market, seize lucrative opportunities, and build a portfolio that stands the test of time. So, are you ready to unlock the secrets of selection and embark on a journey towards real estate success? Let's begin the quest together and uncover the properties that hold the key to your financial prosperity.

"Secrets of Selection: Finding Properties with Maximum Potential" invites you into the inner sanctum of real estate expertise, unveiling the clandestine strategies employed by top performers to uncover hidden gems and capitalize on properties with unparalleled potential. In this pivotal chapter, we delve into the art and science of property selection, equipping you with the tools and insights needed to identify, evaluate, and acquire properties that promise maximum returns.

At its essence, property selection is not merely about finding any property; it's about finding the right property—the one that aligns perfectly with your investment goals, risk tolerance, and long-term vision. We begin by elucidating the importance of defining clear investment criteria, whether it's targeting specific geographic locations, property types, or financial metrics. By establishing precise parameters, you'll streamline your search process and focus your efforts on properties that meet your exacting standards.

Moreover, we explore the multifaceted factors that contribute to a property's potential value appreciation. Beyond just location and physical attributes, we delve into qualitative considerations such as neighborhood dynamics, market demand, and future development prospects. Through in-depth case studies and expert analysis, we illustrate how to identify properties poised for growth and profitability, even in competitive markets.

In addition to traditional methods of property selection, we also shed light on innovative approaches and unconventional sources of opportunity. From distressed properties and off-market deals to creative financing structures and value-add strategies, we uncover the hidden niches and untapped potentials that lie beneath the surface of the real estate market. By thinking outside the box and embracing strategic creativity, you'll unlock new avenues for generating value and maximizing returns on your investments.

Furthermore, we delve into the intricacies of due diligence and property evaluation, ensuring that you have the tools and techniques needed to conduct thorough assessments and mitigate risks. Whether it's analyzing financial statements, inspecting physical condition, or assessing market comparables, we provide you with a comprehensive framework for making informed decisions and minimizing potential pitfalls.

Deal-Making Dynamics

By the end of this chapter, you'll emerge with a newfound mastery of deal-making dynamics and the confidence to negotiate with skill and precision. Armed with these strategies and insights, you'll be well-equipped to navigate the complexities of real estate negotiations, seize opportunities, and drive maximum value in every deal. So, are you ready to unlock the secrets of negotiation success and elevate your real estate game to new heights? Let's dive in and master the art of the deal together.

This chapter opens the door to the art of negotiation, a critical skill set that separates the ordinary from the extraordinary in the world of real estate. In this chapter, we delve into the intricacies of negotiation, equipping you with the strategies, tactics, and mindset needed to secure favorable deals and drive maximum value in every transaction.

Negotiation is more than just a transactional exchange of offers and counteroffers; it's a strategic dance that requires finesse, preparation, and adaptability. We begin by laying the groundwork for effective negotiation, emphasizing the importance of preparation, information gathering, and understanding the motivations and interests of all parties involved. By arming yourself with knowledge and insight, you'll be better equipped to navigate the negotiation process with confidence and poise.

Moreover, we explore the psychology of negotiation and the power dynamics at play. From building rapport and establishing trust to managing emotions and overcoming objections, we provide you with a comprehensive toolkit for fostering constructive dialogue and reaching mutually beneficial agreements. Whether you're negotiating with sellers, buyers, investors, or lenders, mastering the art of persuasion and influence is key to achieving your desired outcomes.

In addition to interpersonal dynamics, we delve into the strategic aspects of negotiation, including setting ambitious but realistic goals, creating leverage through alternative options, and employing creative problem-solving techniques to overcome impasses. Through real-world examples and case studies, we illustrate how top performers leverage their negotiation prowess to secure favorable terms, whether it's price concessions, favorable financing, or additional incentives.

Furthermore, we explore the importance of negotiation ethics and integrity in building long-term relationships and preserving your reputation in the industry. While it's important to advocate for your interests and drive a hard bargain, doing so with integrity and respect for all parties involved is paramount to fostering trust and goodwill in the real estate community.

The Power of Partnerships

By the end of this chapter, you'll emerge with a deep appreciation for the power of partnerships and the transformative impact they can have on your real estate endeavors. Armed with this knowledge, you'll be well-equipped to identify strategic opportunities for collaboration, forge meaningful partnerships, and unlock new levels of profitability and success in the dynamic world of real estate. So, are you ready to harness the power of partnerships and take your real estate business to new heights? Let's explore the possibilities together and unlock the full potential of collaboration.

"The Power of Partnerships: Collaborating for Greater Profitability" unveils the transformative potential inherent in forging strategic alliances and collaborative ventures within the realm of real estate. In this chapter, we explore how partnerships can amplify profitability, mitigate risk, and unlock new opportunities for growth and success.

At its core, the power of partnerships lies in synergy—the combined strengths, resources, and expertise of multiple parties working towards a common goal. We begin by dissecting the various forms of partnerships prevalent in real estate, from joint ventures and syndications to strategic alliances and co-investing arrangements. By understanding the different partnership structures available, you'll be better equipped to identify opportunities for collaboration that align with your investment objectives and risk profile.

Moreover, we delve into the benefits of partnerships beyond just financial gain.

Collaborating with like-minded individuals or entities can provide access to specialized knowledge, networks, and resources that may otherwise be out of reach. Whether it's tapping into a partner's expertise in a specific market or leveraging their access to off-market deals, partnerships offer a myriad of strategic advantages that can accelerate your success in real estate.

In addition to enhancing profitability, partnerships also offer a means of mitigating risk and diversifying your investment portfolio. By spreading risk across multiple parties and assets, you can minimize exposure to market fluctuations, unforeseen challenges, and individual property-specific risks. Furthermore, partnerships can provide access to larger-scale projects and investment opportunities that may be beyond the reach of individual investors, enabling you to capitalize on economies of scale and unlock new avenues for growth.

Furthermore, we explore the importance of trust, communication, and alignment of interests in fostering successful partnerships. Clear communication, mutual respect, and a shared vision are essential ingredients for building strong and resilient partnerships that stand the test of time. By cultivating trust and transparency in your partnerships, you'll lay the foundation for long-term collaboration and mutual success.

From Acquisition to Activation

By the end of this chapter, you'll emerge with a comprehensive understanding of the journey from acquisition to activation and the strategies required to turn properties into profitable assets. Armed with this knowledge, you'll be well-equipped to navigate the complexities of real estate investing, seize opportunities for value creation, and achieve sustainable success in the dynamic world of real estate. So, are you ready to unlock the full potential of your properties and turn them into engines of profitability? Let's embark on this transformative journey together and unleash the power of real estate investment.

This is the pivotal stage where real estate ventures transform from mere investments into lucrative revenue streams. In this chapter, we delve into the intricacies of the property lifecycle, guiding you through the process of maximizing profitability at every stage, from acquisition to activation.

Acquisition marks the starting point of the journey, where properties are identified, evaluated, and ultimately secured. We begin by exploring the strategies and techniques for sourcing potential properties, whether through traditional channels such as MLS listings or more unconventional avenues like off-market deals and distressed sales. By honing your skills in property selection and due diligence, you'll be better equipped to identify opportunities that align with your investment objectives and offer the potential for long-term growth and profitability.

Once a property is acquired, the focus shifts to activation—the process of unlocking its full potential and generating returns. We delve into the various strategies and tactics for optimizing property performance, whether through renovation, repositioning, or redevelopment. By enhancing the value proposition of the property through strategic improvements and upgrades, you'll not only attract higher-quality tenants but also command premium rental rates and increase overall profitability.

Moreover, we explore the importance of effective property management in maximizing returns and mitigating risks. From tenant screening and lease administration to maintenance and operations, diligent property management is essential for preserving asset value and ensuring a steady stream of income. By implementing systems and processes that streamline operations and enhance tenant satisfaction, you'll lay the foundation for long-term success and sustainability in the real estate market.

In addition to traditional rental income, we also explore alternative revenue streams and value-added opportunities that can further enhance profitability. This includes exploring options such as short-term rentals, vacation properties, and ancillary services like parking, storage, and amenities. By diversifying your revenue streams and tapping into emerging trends, you'll position yourself for greater resilience and profitability in an ever-evolving market landscape.

Furthermore, we delve into the importance of exit strategies and portfolio optimization in maximizing overall returns. Whether it's through refinancing, portfolio rebalancing, or strategic divestment, having a clear plan for exit ensures that you can capitalize on opportunities for value realization and reinvestment, thereby maximizing long-term wealth accumulation and portfolio growth.

Revenue Streams Unveiled

By the end of this chapter, you'll emerge with a comprehensive understanding of the diverse income sources available within the real estate industry and the strategies required to capitalize on them. Armed with this knowledge, you'll be well-equipped to diversify your revenue streams, mitigate risk, and maximize profitability in your real estate ventures. So, are you ready to unveil the hidden potential of diverse income sources and unlock new opportunities for financial growth and success? Let's explore the possibilities together and harness the power of diverse revenue streams in real estate.

"Revenue Streams Unveiled: Exploring Diverse Income Sources" lifts the veil on the multitude of income avenues within the real estate industry, providing a comprehensive guide to diversifying your revenue streams and maximizing profitability. In this chapter, we embark on a journey to uncover the myriad ways in which real estate investors can generate income beyond traditional rental returns, unlocking untapped potential and expanding your financial horizons.

While rental income may be the cornerstone of real estate investing, it's just one piece of the puzzle. We begin by exploring alternative income sources that can complement and augment your rental earnings. This includes strategies such as short-term rentals, vacation properties, and corporate housing, which offer the potential for higher cash flow and increased flexibility compared to long-term leases. By tapping into these emerging trends and niche markets, you'll open up new avenues for generating income and maximizing returns on your investment properties.

Moreover, we delve into ancillary revenue streams and value-added services that can further enhance profitability. From parking and storage to laundry facilities and amenities, there are numerous opportunities to monetize additional services and amenities that enhance the tenant experience and add value to your properties. By leveraging these ancillary revenue streams, you'll not only increase cash flow but also improve the overall attractiveness and competitiveness of your properties in the market.

In addition to rental and ancillary income, we explore the potential for passive income through real estate investment vehicles such as real estate investment trusts (REITs), real estate crowdfunding platforms, and syndications. These investment vehicles offer investors the opportunity to passively invest in diversified real estate portfolios or specific projects without the day-to-day responsibilities of property ownership. By diversifying your investment portfolio with these passive income streams, you'll spread risk and potentially achieve higher returns with lower capital requirements and management overhead.

Furthermore, we delve into creative financing strategies and debt instruments that can generate income through interest payments, loan origination fees, and other financing-related activities. Whether it's through private lending, seller financing, or mortgage note investing, there are numerous opportunities to generate passive income through lending and debt investments within the real estate industry.

Risk Management Redefined

By the end of this chapter, you'll emerge with a redefined perspective on risk management and the strategies required to navigate the complexities of the real estate market with confidence and resilience. Armed with this knowledge, you'll be well-equipped to identify, assess, and mitigate risks effectively, ensuring the long-term success and sustainability of your real estate investments. So, are you ready to redefine risk management and take control of your real estate destiny? Let's embark on this transformative journey together and unlock new levels of success in the face of uncertainty.

This chapter reshapes the conventional understanding of risk within the real estate industry, offering a comprehensive framework for identifying, assessing, and mitigating potential challenges and uncertainties. In this chapter, we embark on a journey to redefine risk management as a proactive strategy for safeguarding your investments and maximizing long-term success.

At its core, risk management in real estate involves more than just avoiding or minimizing risk—it's about understanding, quantifying, and strategically managing risk to optimize returns and achieve your investment objectives. We begin by dissecting the various types of risks inherent in real estate investing, from market fluctuations and economic downturns to property-specific risks such as vacancies, tenant defaults, and physical damage.

Moreover, we explore the importance of risk assessment and due diligence in the investment decision-making process. Whether you're evaluating potential properties, assessing financing options, or analyzing market trends, conducting thorough due diligence is essential for identifying potential pitfalls and mitigating risk. By employing rigorous analytical techniques and leveraging expert insights, you'll be better equipped to make informed decisions and safeguard your investments against unforeseen challenges.

In addition to property-specific risks, we delve into broader macroeconomic factors and market dynamics that can impact real estate investments. From interest rate fluctuations and regulatory changes to demographic shifts and geopolitical uncertainties, external factors can have a significant impact on property values and investment returns. By staying informed and actively monitoring market trends, you'll be better prepared to adapt to changing conditions and mitigate the impact of external risks on your investment portfolio.

Furthermore, we explore the importance of diversification as a risk management strategy. By spreading your investments across different asset classes, geographic locations, and property types, you can reduce exposure to individual risks and enhance overall portfolio resilience. Whether it's through diversifying across property sectors, investment strategies, or financing sources, diversification is a powerful tool for mitigating risk and protecting your wealth against market downturns and volatility.

Moreover, we delve into the role of insurance and risk transfer mechanisms in real estate risk management. From property insurance and liability coverage to title insurance and warranty programs, insurance products can provide an additional layer of protection against unforeseen events and liabilities. By understanding your insurance options and securing appropriate coverage, you can minimize financial exposure and mitigate potential losses in the event of accidents, disasters, or legal disputes.

Marketing Magic: Techniques for Effective Property Promotion

By the end of this chapter, you'll emerge with a comprehensive understanding of the magic behind effective property promotion and the strategies required to captivate audiences, generate interest, and drive action. Armed with this knowledge, you'll be well-equipped to create compelling marketing campaigns that elevate your properties above the competition and attract qualified buyers or tenants. So, are you ready to unlock the secrets of marketing magic and unleash the full potential of your real estate ventures? Let's dive into the enchanting world of property promotion and make your properties shine.

Here we unveil the spellbinding strategies and techniques essential for captivating potential buyers or tenants and maximizing the visibility and desirability of your properties. In this chapter, we immerse ourselves in the art and science of real estate marketing, empowering you to craft compelling narratives, leverage cutting-edge tactics, and harness the power of digital and traditional channels to showcase your properties in the best light possible.

At its core, effective property promotion is about more than just listing a property—it's about telling a captivating story that resonates with your target audience and showcases the unique value proposition of your property. We begin by exploring the importance of branding and positioning in creating a distinctive identity for your properties, whether it's through compelling visuals, engaging narratives, or strategic messaging that highlights key features and benefits.

Let's delve into the various channels and mediums available for property promotion, from digital platforms such as websites, social media, and online listings to traditional channels such as print advertising, signage, and direct mail. By leveraging a multi-channel marketing approach, you'll reach a broader audience and maximize exposure for your properties, increasing the likelihood of attracting qualified leads and generating interest.

In addition to broad-reaching marketing campaigns, we explore the importance of targeted marketing strategies that speak directly to your ideal buyers or tenants. Whether it's through demographic targeting, geographic segmentation, or psychographic profiling, understanding the preferences and needs of your target audience enables you to tailor your marketing efforts for maximum impact and effectiveness.

Furthermore, we delve into the role of technology and innovation in revolutionizing real estate marketing. From immersive virtual tours and 3D renderings to drone photography and augmented reality, cutting-edge technologies offer new ways to showcase properties and engage buyers or tenants in immersive and interactive experiences. By embracing these innovative tools and techniques, you'll differentiate your properties from the competition and leave a lasting impression on potential clients.

Moreover, we explore the importance of measurement and analytics in assessing the effectiveness of your marketing efforts and refining your strategies for optimal results. By tracking key performance indicators such as website traffic, lead generation, and conversion rates, you'll gain valuable insights into what's working and what's not, enabling you to iterate and optimize your marketing campaigns for greater success.

Customer Connection

By the end of this chapter, you'll emerge with a deep appreciation for the importance of customer connection in driving repeat success in the real estate industry. Armed with the strategies and insights shared in this chapter, you'll be well-equipped to cultivate lasting relationships with clients, generate repeat business, and earn referrals that fuel long-term growth and success in your real estate endeavors. So, are you ready to embark on the journey of creating lasting connections with your clients and unlocking the keys to repeat success? Let's build relationships that stand the test of time and lead to unparalleled success in the world of real estate.

This chapter goes beyond mere transactions, emphasizing the importance of fostering genuine connections, delivering exceptional service, and nurturing trust to cultivate a loyal client base that leads to repeat business and referrals.

At its core, customer connection is about more than just closing deals—it's about understanding the needs, preferences, and aspirations of your clients and creating meaningful experiences that resonate with them on a personal level. We begin by exploring the foundational principles of customer-centricity and empathy, emphasizing the importance of active listening, genuine empathy, and a client-first mentality in building rapport and establishing trust.

Also, we delve into the various touchpoints and interactions throughout the customer journey, from initial contact and property tours to negotiation, closing, and beyond. At each stage, we explore strategies for delivering exceptional service, exceeding expectations, and adding value to the client experience. Whether it's providing personalized recommendations, offering expert guidance, or anticipating needs before they arise, every interaction is an opportunity to deepen the connection and strengthen the relationship with your clients.

In addition to providing outstanding service, we explore the importance of transparency and communication in building trust and credibility with clients. By keeping clients informed and involved throughout the process, you'll foster a sense of transparency and openness that instills confidence and reassurance in their decision-making. Moreover, we explore the role of honesty and integrity in building lasting relationships, emphasizing the importance of ethical conduct and always putting the client's best interests first.

Furthermore, we delve into the power of follow-up and ongoing communication in maintaining relationships and fostering loyalty over time. Whether it's sending personalized thank-you notes, providing market updates, or hosting client appreciation events, staying top-of-mind and demonstrating ongoing value ensures that clients remain engaged and connected even after the transaction is complete.

Moreover, we explore the importance of leveraging technology and automation to enhance the customer experience and streamline communication. From CRM systems and email marketing platforms to social media engagement and personalized content, technology offers powerful tools for staying connected with clients and delivering tailored experiences that resonate with their individual needs and preferences.

Innovation Incubator

By the end of this chapter, you'll emerge with a comprehensive understanding of the transformative potential of technology in advancing the real estate industry and the strategies required to embrace innovation and drive real estate advancement. Armed with this knowledge, you'll be well-equipped to leverage technology as a catalyst for growth, differentiation, and success in your real estate endeavors. So, are you ready to step into the innovation incubator and harness the power of technology to propel your real estate business to new heights? Let's embark on this transformative journey together and unlock the endless possibilities of real estate innovation.

Innovation Incubator delves into the transformative role of technology in revolutionizing the real estate industry and empowering professionals to adapt, innovate, and thrive in an increasingly digital world. This chapter serves as a guide to harnessing the power of technology to streamline processes, enhance efficiency, and unlock new opportunities for growth and success.

At its core, the innovation incubator is about more than just adopting the latest gadgets or software—it's about embracing a culture of innovation and leveraging technology as a strategic enabler to drive real estate advancement. We begin by exploring the myriad ways in which technology is reshaping the real estate landscape, from artificial intelligence and big data analytics to virtual reality and blockchain technology. By understanding the potential of these emerging technologies, you'll be better equipped to identify opportunities for innovation and stay ahead of the curve in a rapidly evolving industry.

Moreover, we delve into the practical applications of technology across various aspects of the real estate lifecycle, from property acquisition and development to marketing, sales, and property management. Whether it's using predictive analytics to identify investment opportunities, leveraging virtual staging and 3D tours to showcase properties, or implementing smart home technology to enhance tenant satisfaction, technology offers countless opportunities to optimize processes, improve decision-making, and deliver superior value to clients and stakeholders.

In addition to enhancing operational efficiency and client experience, we explore the role of technology in driving sustainability and environmental responsibility within the real estate industry. From energy-efficient building systems and green construction materials to smart grid technology and renewable energy solutions, technology offers innovative ways to reduce environmental impact and create more sustainable, resilient built environments for future generations.

Furthermore, we delve into the importance of digital transformation and organizational agility in adapting to the changing demands of the market. Whether you're a solo agent, a small brokerage, or a large real estate firm, embracing technology and fostering a culture of innovation is essential for staying competitive and future-proofing your business in an increasingly digital and interconnected world.

Growing Your Portfolio with Precision

By the end of this chapter, you'll emerge with a comprehensive understanding of scaling strategies and the tools and techniques required to grow your real estate portfolio with precision and foresight. Armed with this knowledge, you'll be well-equipped to navigate the complexities of portfolio growth, seize opportunities for expansion, and achieve sustainable success in the dynamic world of real estate investing. So, are you ready to scale your portfolio with precision and unlock new levels of growth and prosperity? Let's embark on this transformative journey together and elevate your real estate business to new heights.

Scaling Strategies: Growing Your Portfolio with Precision serves as a roadmap for real estate professionals seeking to expand their portfolios strategically and sustainably. This chapter delves into the intricacies of scaling, providing insights, techniques, and best practices to navigate the challenges and capitalize on the opportunities inherent in portfolio growth.

At its core, scaling in real estate is about more than just acquiring more properties—it's about expanding your portfolio with precision, efficiency, and foresight. We begin by exploring the foundational principles of scaling, emphasizing the importance of setting clear goals, defining investment criteria, and developing a strategic roadmap for growth. By establishing a solid foundation and vision for your portfolio, you'll lay the groundwork for success and ensure that every acquisition moves you closer to your long-term objectives.

Moreover, we delve into the various strategies and approaches for scaling your portfolio, from organic growth and property development to acquisitions, partnerships, and syndications. Whether you're looking to diversify your holdings, enter new markets, or expand your asset classes, understanding the different scaling strategies available enables you to tailor your approach to fit your unique circumstances, risk tolerance, and investment goals.

In addition to strategic planning, we explore the importance of financial management and risk mitigation in scaling your portfolio. From securing financing and managing leverage to conducting thorough due diligence and risk assessment, prudent financial management is essential for safeguarding your investments and ensuring sustainable growth over time. By implementing sound financial practices and risk mitigation strategies, you'll mitigate potential pitfalls and position your portfolio for long-term success and resilience.

Furthermore, we delve into the role of systems, processes, and scalability in supporting portfolio growth. Whether it's implementing technology solutions to streamline operations, building a team of professionals to support your efforts, or establishing standardized procedures for property management and asset optimization, having scalable systems in place is essential for managing complexity and maintaining efficiency as your portfolio expands.

Also, we explore the importance of agility and adaptability in scaling your portfolio in response to changing market conditions and emerging trends. Whether it's seizing opportunities in a shifting market, pivoting your strategy in response to new regulations, or capitalizing on emerging investment trends, staying nimble and flexible enables you to capitalize on opportunities and navigate challenges with confidence and resilience.

Financial Fitness

By the end of this chapter, you'll emerge with a comprehensive understanding of financial fitness and the strategies required to optimize resources, maximize returns, and build long-term wealth in real estate investing. Armed with this knowledge, you'll be well-equipped to navigate the complexities of financial management, make informed decisions, and achieve your financial goals with confidence and precision. So, are you ready to embark on the journey of financial fitness and unlock the keys to long-term wealth and prosperity? Let's begin the transformation together and build a solid financial future in the world of real estate investing.

Let's explore the essential principles and practices of financial management within the realm of real estate investing. This chapter serves as a comprehensive guide to optimizing resources, maximizing returns, and building long-term wealth through strategic financial planning and management.

At its core, financial fitness in real estate is about more than just maximizing short-term profits—it's about building a solid financial foundation and implementing strategies that promote sustainable growth and wealth accumulation over the long term. We begin by exploring the fundamental principles of financial fitness, including budgeting, saving, investing, and debt management. By mastering these core principles, you'll lay the groundwork for sound financial decision-making and long-term success in real estate investing.

Moreover, we delve into the various financial strategies and techniques for optimizing resources and maximizing returns on investment properties. This includes exploring options such as leveraging other people's money (OPM) through financing, optimizing cash flow through strategic rental pricing and expense management, and maximizing tax efficiency through proper structuring and deductions. By implementing these strategies effectively, you'll optimize returns, mitigate risks, and enhance overall portfolio performance.

In addition to traditional financial management techniques, we explore the importance of asset protection and estate planning in safeguarding your wealth and securing your legacy for future generations. Whether it's through insurance, trusts, or entity structuring, protecting your assets from unforeseen liabilities and ensuring a smooth transfer of wealth requires careful planning and consideration. By implementing proactive asset protection and estate planning strategies, you'll safeguard your wealth and provide for your loved ones long into the future.

Furthermore, we delve into the role of financial education and continuous learning in achieving financial fitness and success in real estate investing. Whether it's staying abreast of market trends, expanding your knowledge of investment strategies, or honing your financial skills through workshops and seminars, ongoing education is essential for staying competitive and maximizing opportunities in the ever-evolving real estate landscape.

Moreover, we explore the importance of mindset and behavior in achieving financial fitness and success. From cultivating a mindset of abundance and wealth consciousness to practicing discipline and delayed gratification, adopting healthy financial habits and behaviors is essential for achieving long-term financial goals and building lasting wealth in real estate.

Legacy Planning: Building a Sustainable Real Estate Empire

By the end of this chapter, you'll emerge with a comprehensive understanding of legacy planning and the strategies required to build a sustainable real estate empire that stands the test of time. Armed with this knowledge, you'll be well-equipped to define your legacy, cultivate a vision for the future, and create a lasting impact that transcends generations. So, are you ready to embark on the journey of legacy planning and build a real estate empire that leaves a profound and enduring mark on the world? Let's begin the journey together and create a legacy that lasts for generations to come.

This chapter embodies the vision and foresight required to establish a lasting impact in the realm of real estate. It is a blueprint for creating a sustainable legacy that transcends generations, leaving a profound mark on the industry and the communities it serves.

At its essence, legacy planning in real estate is about more than just amassing wealth—it's about stewardship, vision, and a commitment to creating lasting value for future generations. We begin by exploring the foundational principles of legacy planning, emphasizing the importance of defining your purpose, values, and vision for your real estate empire. By articulating a clear mission and legacy, you'll align your actions and decisions with a higher purpose, guiding the growth and evolution of your empire over time.

Moreover, we delve into the various strategies and techniques for building a sustainable real estate empire that stands the test of time. This includes exploring options such as portfolio diversification, asset optimization, and strategic partnerships to maximize resilience and adaptability in a changing market landscape. By building a diverse and resilient portfolio, you'll mitigate risk, capitalize on opportunities, and ensure the longevity and sustainability of your empire for generations to come.

In addition to financial considerations, we explore the importance of social responsibility and community impact in legacy planning. Whether it's through sustainable development practices, community engagement initiatives, or philanthropic endeavors, integrating social and environmental considerations into your business model is essential for creating a legacy that extends beyond financial wealth and leaves a positive impact on society and the environment.

Furthermore, we delve into the role of succession planning and leadership development in ensuring the continuity and growth of your real estate empire beyond your lifetime. By grooming the next generation of leaders and empowering them with the skills, knowledge, and values needed to carry forward your legacy, you'll ensure that your vision and impact endure long into the future.

Also, we explore the importance of storytelling and communication in shaping and preserving your legacy. By documenting your journey, sharing your experiences, and articulating your vision for the future, you'll inspire others to carry forward your legacy and uphold the values and principles that define your real estate empire.

The Road Ahead

By the end of this chapter, you'll emerge with a comprehensive understanding of the road ahead and the strategies required to adapt and thrive in an ever-changing market environment. Armed with this knowledge, you'll be well-equipped to navigate uncertainty, seize opportunities, and build a successful and resilient real estate business in the years to come. So, are you ready to embrace the road ahead and chart a course for success in the dynamic world of real estate? Let's embark on this journey together and navigate the future with confidence and resilience.

The Road Ahead: Adapting to Evolving Trends and Markets serves as a compass for navigating the ever-changing landscape of the real estate industry. In this chapter, we explore the dynamic forces shaping the future of real estate and provide insights, strategies, and best practices for staying agile, resilient, and ahead of the curve in a rapidly evolving market environment.

At its core, adapting to evolving trends and markets is about more than just reacting to change—it's about anticipating shifts, embracing innovation, and proactively positioning yourself for success in a constantly evolving landscape. We begin by exploring the key trends and megatrends shaping the future of real estate, from demographic shifts and technological advancements to environmental sustainability and urbanization. By understanding these trends and their potential implications, you'll be better equipped to identify opportunities and mitigate risks in an uncertain future.

Moreover, we delve into the importance of continuous learning and adaptation in staying relevant and competitive in the real estate industry. Whether it's staying abreast of emerging technologies, trends, and market dynamics, or honing your skills and expertise through professional development and education, ongoing learning is essential for staying ahead of the curve and capitalizing on new opportunities as they arise.

In addition to staying informed, we explore the importance of innovation and creativity in driving success in a rapidly changing market landscape. Whether it's embracing new technologies such as artificial intelligence, blockchain, and virtual reality, or adopting innovative business models and strategies, embracing innovation enables you to differentiate yourself, create value, and stay ahead of the competition in an increasingly competitive market environment.

Furthermore, we delve into the importance of adaptability and resilience in navigating market volatility and uncertainty. Whether it's through diversifying your portfolio, maintaining liquidity, or developing contingency plans for unforeseen events, being agile and adaptable enables you to weather storms, capitalize on opportunities, and thrive in the face of adversity.

We also explore the importance of collaboration and partnerships in navigating complex market dynamics and driving collective success. Whether it's partnering with other industry stakeholders, forming strategic alliances, or collaborating with technology providers and startups, leveraging the power of networks and ecosystems enables you to access new opportunities, resources, and insights that can accelerate your growth and success in the real estate industry.

Reflections from the Top Performers in Real Estate

By the end of this chapter, readers will gain a deeper appreciation for the insights and wisdom shared by top performers in the real estate industry. Armed with this knowledge, inspiration, and guidance, we are empowered to embark on our own journey to success, equipped with the tools, strategies, and mindset needed to thrive in the dynamic and rewarding world of real estate. So, as we conclude this book, let us carry forward the lessons learned and the wisdom gained, as we strive to achieve our own success and make a positive impact in the world of real estate.

"Reflections from the Top Performers in Real Estate" offers invaluable insights and wisdom distilled from the experiences of industry leaders and top performers who have achieved remarkable success in the real estate world. In this final chapter, we pause to reflect on the lessons learned, the challenges overcome, and the strategies employed by those who have risen to the pinnacle of success in the real estate industry.

At its essence, the closing thoughts chapter serves as a repository of wisdom—a collection of reflections, anecdotes, and pearls of wisdom from those who have walked the path before us. We begin by delving into the personal journeys and professional trajectories of top performers, exploring the defining moments, pivotal decisions, and hard-earned lessons that have shaped their success. By learning from their experiences and insights, we gain valuable perspective and inspiration to guide our own journey in the real estate industry.

Moreover, we explore the common characteristics and traits shared by top performers in real estate, from resilience and perseverance to adaptability, innovation, and a relentless pursuit of excellence. By understanding the mindset and qualities that set top performers apart, we gain valuable insights into what it takes to succeed in a competitive and dynamic industry.

In addition to personal reflections, we delve into the strategies and tactics employed by top performers to achieve exceptional results in their real estate endeavors. Whether it's mastering the art of negotiation, building strong relationships with clients, or leveraging technology and innovation to gain a competitive edge, we uncover the keys to their success and distill actionable insights that can be applied to our own real estate practice.

Furthermore, we explore the importance of mentorship and learning from others in accelerating our growth and development in the real estate industry. Whether it's seeking guidance from seasoned professionals, joining mastermind groups, or investing in continuing education and professional development, surrounding ourselves with mentors and peers who have achieved success can provide invaluable support, guidance, and inspiration on our journey to the top.

we also reflect on the broader significance of real estate as a vehicle for wealth creation, community development, and societal impact. From providing homes for families and creating vibrant communities to driving economic growth and prosperity, real estate plays a pivotal role in shaping the world around us. By recognizing the broader purpose and impact of our work, we gain a deeper sense of fulfillment and purpose in our real estate endeavors.

Conclusion

In closing, "The Insider's Guide to Real Estate Success: Secrets of Top Performers Revealed" has been a journey of discovery, empowerment, and transformation in the realm of real estate. Throughout these pages, we have explored the essential strategies, techniques, and insights that have propelled top performers to achieve remarkable success in the industry.

From unlocking the door to insider real estate strategies and mastering the mindset of a top performer to navigating market trends, seizing opportunities, and building lasting relationships with clients, each chapter has provided valuable guidance and inspiration for aspiring real estate professionals.

We have delved into the art of analysis, the secrets of property selection, the dynamics of deal-making, and the power of partnerships—unveiling the strategies and tactics employed by top performers to maximize profitability, mitigate risks, and drive success in their real estate ventures.

Moreover, we have explored the transformative role of technology, the importance of financial fitness, and the strategies for scaling portfolios and building sustainable real estate empires. We have learned from the experiences and reflections of industry leaders, gaining invaluable insights and wisdom that will guide us on our own journey to success.

As we conclude this book, let us carry forward the lessons learned and the wisdom gained, as we embark on our own journey to success in the dynamic and rewarding world of real estate. Let us embrace innovation, adaptability, and resilience, and strive to make a positive impact in the communities we serve.

Whether you are just starting out in the real estate industry or looking to take your business to new heights, remember that success is not merely a destination but a journey—a journey of growth, learning, and continuous improvement. With dedication, perseverance, and a commitment to excellence, you have the power to achieve your goals and create a legacy that will endure for generations to come.

Thank you for joining us on this journey, and may your path to real estate success be filled with prosperity, fulfillment, and abundance.

www.ingramcontent.com/pod-product-compliance
Lightning Source LLC
Chambersburg PA
CBHW070353230526
45471CB00006B/2549